Brain BENDERS

MEGA MAZES

ARCTURUS

This edition published in 2017 by Arcturus Publishing Limited
26/27 Bickels Yard, 151–153 Bermondsey Street,
London SE1 3HA

ISBN: 978-1-78828-063-1
CH005930NT
Supplier 10, Date 0817, Print run 6326

Editorial by JMS llp
Maze Illustrations by Quadrum
Illustrated by Memo Angeles (Shutterstock)
Designed by Mike Reynolds

Printed in the UK

MIX
Paper from
responsible sources
FSC® C018072

CONTENTS

PUZZLE MAZES

Hungry Mouse

Squeak, squeak! Can you guide the mouse to the cheese?

Web Quest

This spider is trying to find his way home! Can you show him the way to his web?

Three Little Pigs

This little pig has lost his friends! Help him make his way through the winding maze to find them again.

Castle Escape!

Robin Hood is trying to find his way out of the castle. Help him escape without coming face-to-face with the knight!

Feeling Nutty

This forgetful squirrel can't remember where he has hidden his nuts. Help him find them again!

Winter Wonderland

Guide these children through the wintry woods to find the snowman. Don't walk into any trees!

Little Red Riding Hood

Can you guide Little Red to her grandmother's house? Doesn't grandma have big teeth!

Elephant

Make a line all the way from the trunk to the tail.

Knight Time!

This knight is racing back to the castle as fast as he can. Can you show him the quickest route?

Give a Dog a Bone

This little dog is feeling hungry! Show him how to get to the bone in the middle of this maze.

Maze Planet

Guide the aliens back to their UFO, so that they can blast off from this maze planet.

Hickory Dickory Dock

The mouse ran up the clock, just not in a straight line!

The Big Chill

Can you show this fisherman how to get home to his igloo?

17

Honeycomb

Dodge the bees to get to the honey!

Journey to the Oasis

Lead this camel to a refreshing drink at the oasis.

Missing Object

This philosopher has lost his most-prized possession—his vase! Can you guide him back to it?

Pirate Treasure

Look at all those gold coins! Help the pirate reach the treasure chest.

21

Kingfisher

Guide the kingfisher through the rippling water, so he can see his next meal.

seahorse

Trace a line from his nose to his tail.

23

Back to the Bat Cave

How good is the bat's homing signal?

Get My Goat

Trace a line from the goat's horn to his tail.

Hungry Caterpillar

Guide this little caterpillar through the maze. When she reaches the middle, she'll turn into a beautiful butterfly!

Cops and Robbers

The chase is on! Guide the police officer through the maze, so that he can catch the burglar.

Starfish

Can you follow a clear path across this starfish?

kangaroo

Draw a line that stretches from the tip of the kangaroo's tail into her pouch.

29

Ostrich

Make your way through the maze from head to tail.

Hopscotch

Hop and jump to the end of this puzzle.

31

Halloween

Carve a route through this scary jack-o'-lantern maze.

Merlin's Hat

Decorate the wizard's hat, as you travel from the brim to the tip.

33

Valentine

Follow the path of
Cupid's arrow.

Blowing Bubbles

This wacky washing machine is making huge soap bubbles! Find your way through them, moving from one end to the other.

Anyone for Tennis?

Help this player do some fancy footwork!

Spiderweb

Lead Sam the spider to his lunch!

Bear and Cub

Connect baby bear's nose to the fish that his mother caught in her mouth.

Reindeer

Draw a line from the tip of one of the reindeer's huge antlers to the other.

Skull and Crossbones

Ahoy there, matey! Can you make it to the treasure before Captain Hook gets his hand on it?

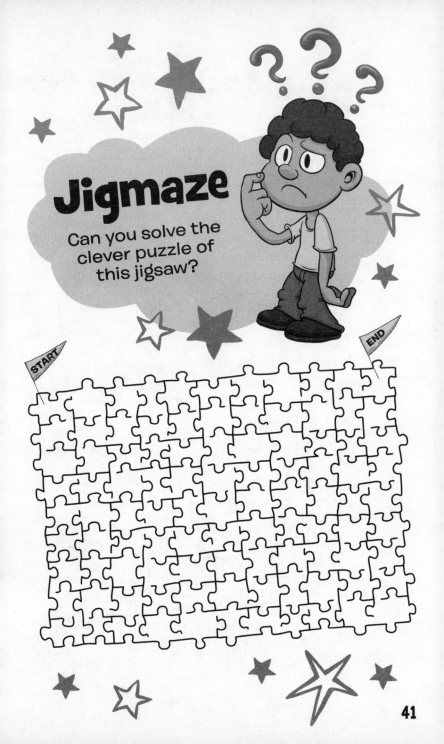

Jigmaze

Can you solve the clever puzzle of this jigsaw?

Diplodocus

This beast has a tiny brain. See how long it takes to get a message to its tail!

Treasure Map

Travel across this island to find your way to Pirate's Bay, where the treasure is buried!

Go Bananas!

Can you find a path from one end of this banana to the other? Don't lose your way, now!

Buffalo Crossing

Trace a line from the buffalo's ear to the songbird on its back!

Mole in a Hole

This mole has hidden a gem in the deepest tunnel of his home. Can you guide him to it?

Golf Club

Putt around this golf course until you exit at the ninth hole.

Snowy Mountain

Help navigate this icy downhill run. It's swift but full of tricky twists!

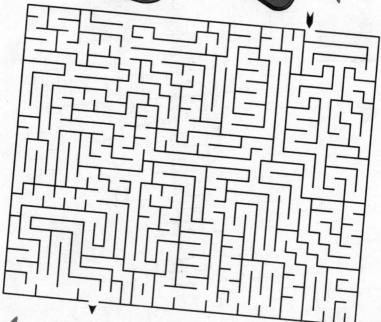

 **FINISH**

Horse Race

Jump for joy if you finish this racecourse without stumbling!

FINISH

City Marathon

Jog along with this runner through the city maze!

FINISH

52

Moonscape

Guide the astronaut back to her spaceship. Make sure she doesn't fall into the craters along the way!

53

Octo-Pirate

This octopus looks well-armed! Guide him to the wheel of the sunken ship.

Whale Tale

Connect the tail of the whale to her waterspout.

Surf's Up!

Help this surfer across the beach, down to the sea.

Labyrinth Challenge

Can you swim through the underwater labyrinth and out the other side?

Fire Rescue!

Lead the way, and help the firefighter put out the flames.

Find the Garage

This old car needs a lot of fixing! Take it to the garage before it breaks down again.

GARAGE

59

CLASSIC LABYRINTH MAZES

Crop Circles

These four odd aliens are racing to the middle of the crop circle. Help them find the right paths to take.

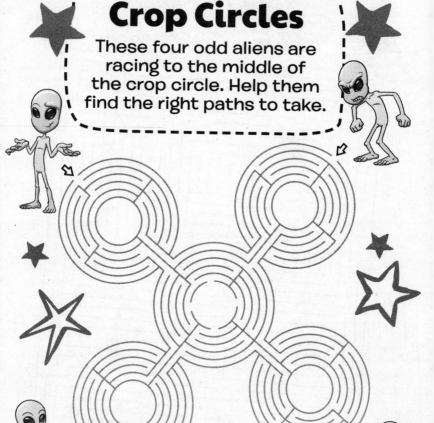

Picnic Pals

Find the yummy food ... but avoid the little pests who want to share your picnic!

Beach Ball

Guide this boy from the middle of the circle to his friends, who are building a sandcastle.

Planting a Tree

Lead these young gardeners to the middle of the tree maze triangle.

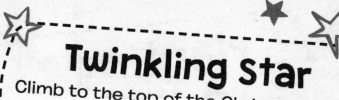

Twinkling star

Climb to the top of the Christmas tree, and make sure the star is straight!

64

Who Let the Dogs Out?

Dogs everywhere! Round up each one, and take them all back to the kennels in one trip.

Island in the Sun

Start in the middle, and pick up the first letter. Then go around the labyrinth, and gather up the other eight letters. In the right order, they will spell a famous island!

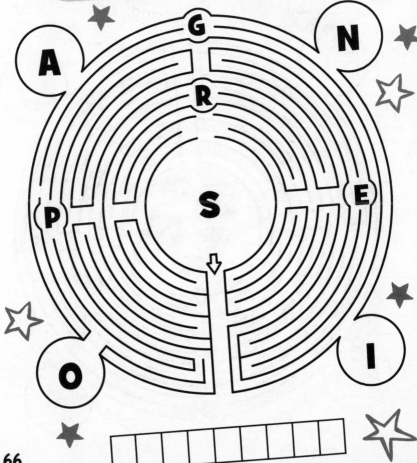

Pretty Pearls

The princess has mixed up her pearl necklaces. How many separate strings are there?

Wizard's Star

Abracadabra! Can you help the wizard reach the middle of this magic labyrinth?

Find the Friends

Three girls are lost in the labyrinth! Start with one arrow at a time, and find the letters of each name in the right order. Then, write their names in the boxes.

Birthday Cake

Find out how steady your hands are! Make a pattern on this birthday cake in one unbroken line.

Treasure Trove

Can you reach the priceless treasure in the middle of this diamond maze?

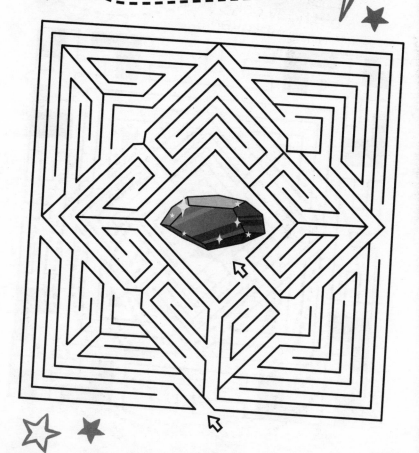

Ancient Temple

This explorer has set off a booby trap. Quick, show her the way out of the temple ... before it collapses!

Stop! Thief!

Help the police dog catch the sneaky thief. You'll have to be quick!

Flower Power

Guide this bee to the beautiful flower.

The Music Goes Around

How will the musical notes escape from this antique gramophone horn? Find out!

In One Ear and Out the Other

Mother Bear claims that everything she says to Baby Bear goes in one ear and out the other. Trace an unbroken line between his ears to find out if it's true!

Lost Boys

Three boys are lost in this labyrinth. Follow one arrow at a time, and find the letters of each of their names in the correct order. Then, write them in the boxes.

The Apple Tree

Trace this ancient tree design, following along the dotted line.

Magic Star

The Good Fairy has recharged her wand with magic stardust. Now she must return to Earth and make some wishes come true. Help her find her way!

TANGLE MAZES

Flying High

The wind has blown these flying objects about and tangled their strings. Can you work out which end belongs to each one?

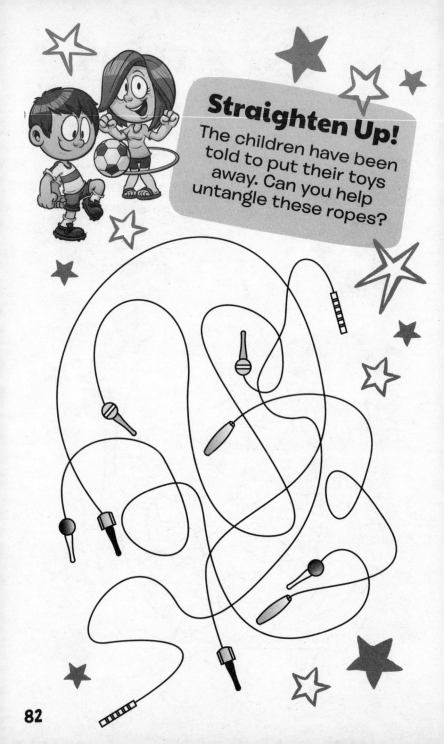

Straighten Up!

The children have been told to put their toys away. Can you help untangle these ropes?

Message in a Bottle

You've found a bottle with a message inside. Which line should you pull to bring the bottle closer to your boat?

Showdown

Five finalists walk their dogs around the dog show. But in their excitement, the leashes have crossed. Match the dogs with their owners.

85

Spaghetti

Dan, Joe, and Will decide to share a plate of spaghetti, but who will get the most?

Slippery Snakes

The zookeeper's assistant has mixed up some snakes. Help her separate them before she gets in trouble!

A Stitch in Time

The strands of threads from these bobbins are in a terrible tangle. Can you get this puzzle sewn up?

Yo-Yo No-No!

The yo-yo contest was going well until someone tried some fancy tricks. Separate the strings so the children can begin again.

A Game of Cricket

If only these crazy cricket players had looked where they were going! Can you help untangle them?

Lost Property

The lost property box is in an awful state. Five pairs of sports shoes are still tied by their shoelaces. Can you trace each shoe to its partner?

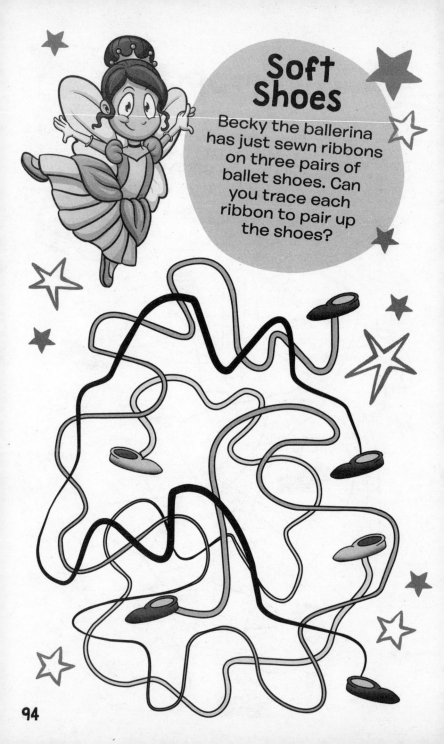

Soft Shoes

Becky the ballerina has just sewn ribbons on three pairs of ballet shoes. Can you trace each ribbon to pair up the shoes?

High Hopes

These children's balloon strings got mixed up at the fair. Can you untangle them before they get home?

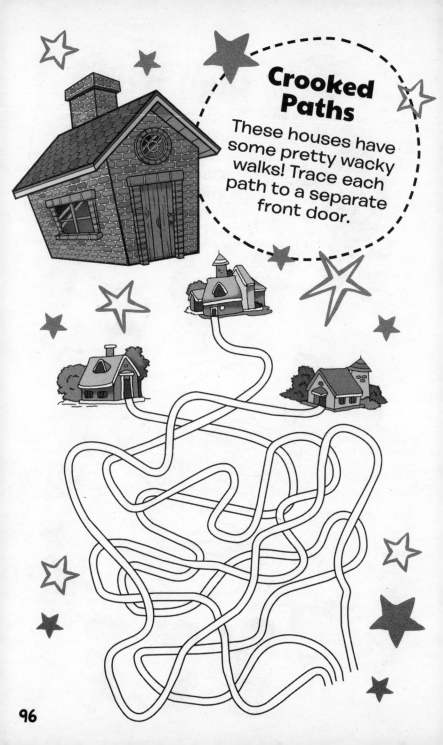

Crooked Paths

These houses have some pretty wacky walks! Trace each path to a separate front door.

Trailing Vines

These grape vines have gone wild! Trace a path from each plant to the grapes.

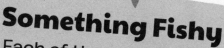

Something Fishy

Each of these fishermen has a bite, but now their lines are tangled up! Can you find out whose fish is whose?

FRACTAL MAZES

Car Dash

Quick, start driving! Help the little car catch the train.

The Hare and the Tortoise

Here they go again! Help the tortoise to find a way to the winning flag.

Lion

Start and finish on the same dot, and carefully move all the way around the lion's mane. Avoid those sharp teeth!

Giraffe

Trace a line from head to tail.

SOLUTIONS

Some of these mazes have multiple routes. We have shown the most common path taken, but you might discover another path which is also correct.

PUZZLE MAZES

Page 4

Page 5

Page 6

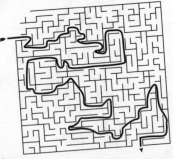

Page 7

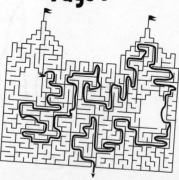

Page 8

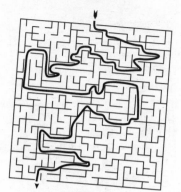

Page 9

Page 10

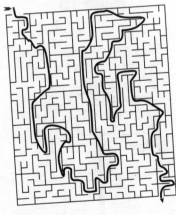

Page 11

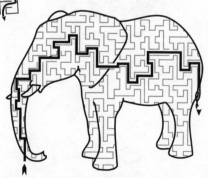

Page 12

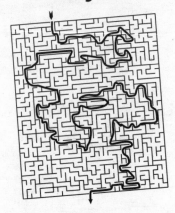

Page 13

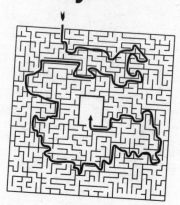

Page 14

Page 15

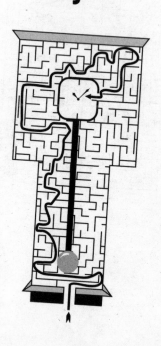

Page 16

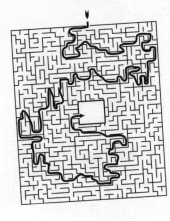

Page 17

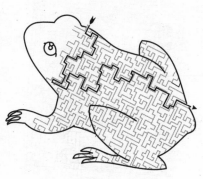

Page 18

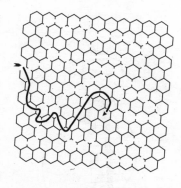

Page 19

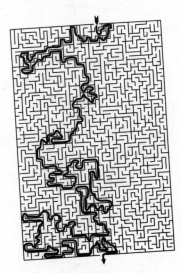

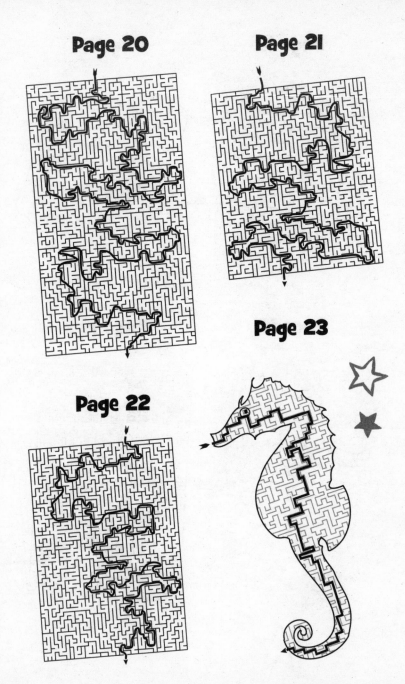

Page 20

Page 21

Page 22

Page 23

Page 24

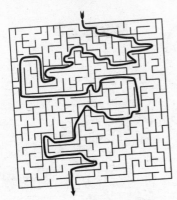

Page 25

Page 26

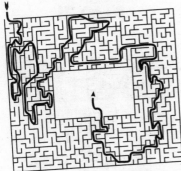

Page 27

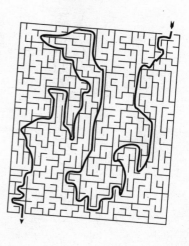

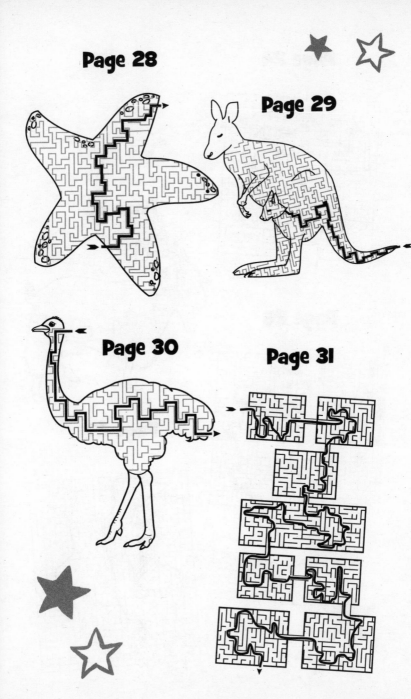

Page 28

Page 29

Page 30

Page 31

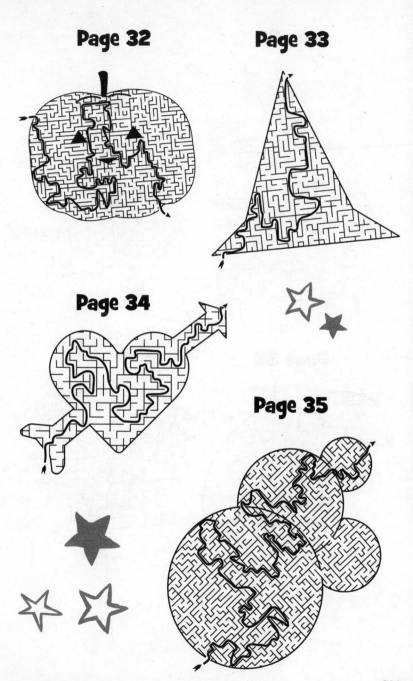

Page 32

Page 33

Page 34

Page 35

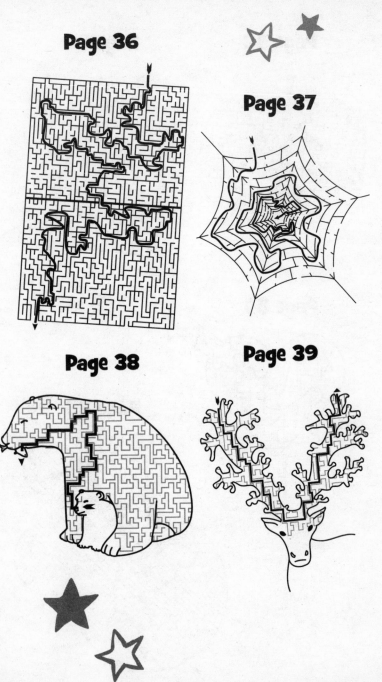

Page 36

Page 37

Page 38

Page 39

Page 40

Page 41

START

END

Page 42

Page 43

Page 44

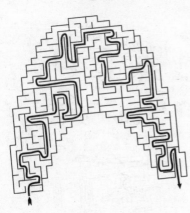

Page 45

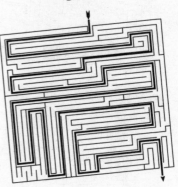

Page 46

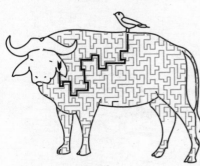

Page 47

Page 48

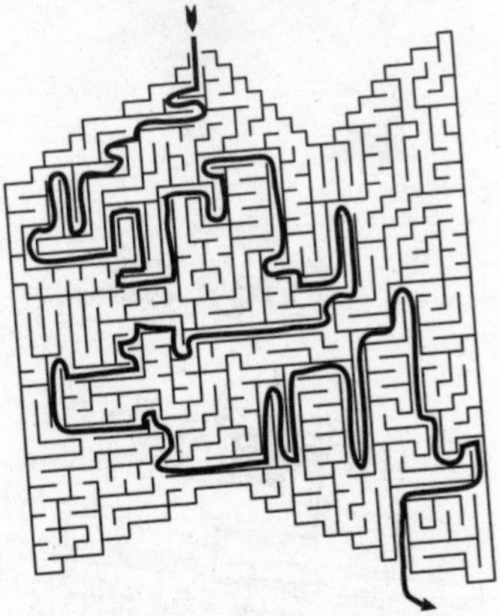

Page 49

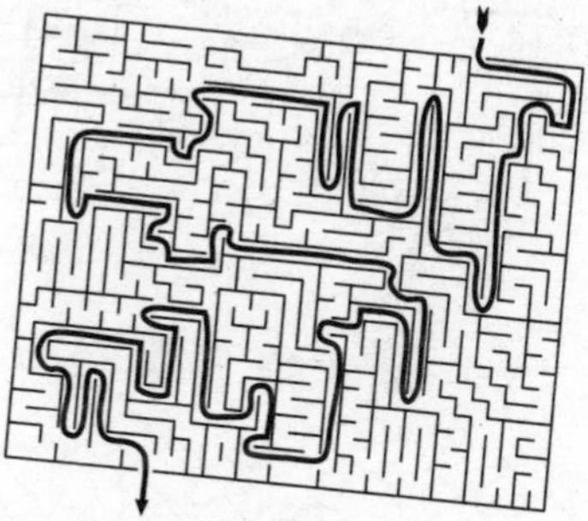

Page 50

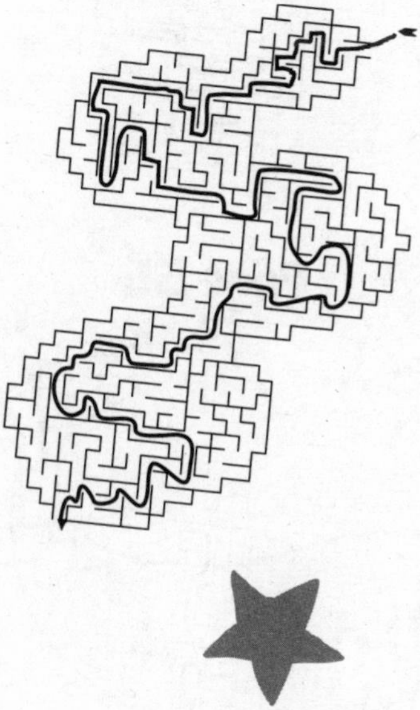

Page 51

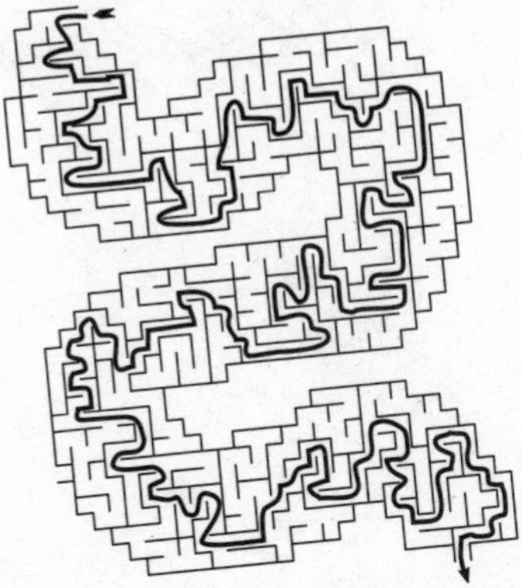

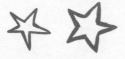

Page 52

Page 53

Page 54

Page 55

Page 56

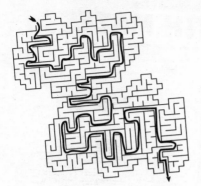

Page 57

Page 58

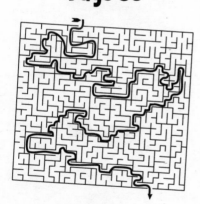

Page 59

CLASSIC LABYRINTH MAZES

Page 60

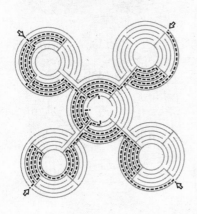

Page 61

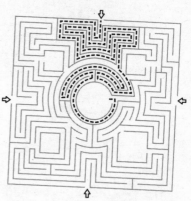

Page 62

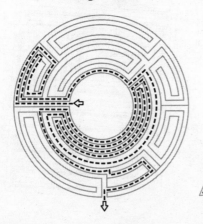

Page 63

Page 64

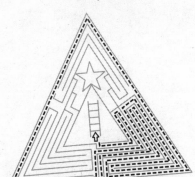

Page 65

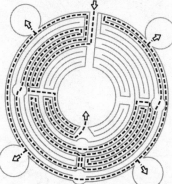

Page 66

SINGAPORE

Page 67

119

Page 68

Page 69

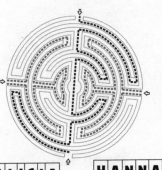

ALICIA   HANNAH
JACQUELINE

Page 70

Page 71

120

Page 72

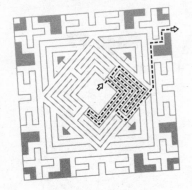

Page 73

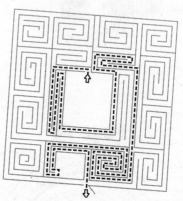

Page 74

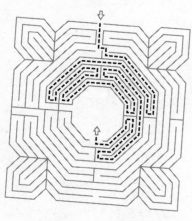

Page 75

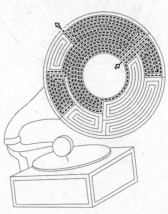

121

Page 76

Page 77

ROGER   DAVID
ALESSANDRO

Page 78

Page 79

TANGLE MAZES

Page 80

Page 81

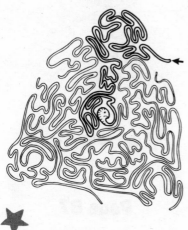

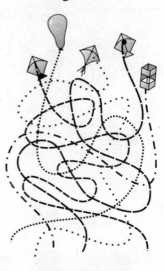

Page 82

Page 83

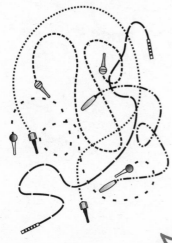

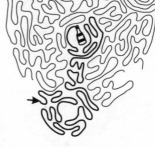

123

Page 84

Page 85

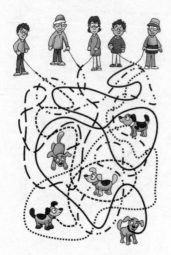

⭐

Page 86

Page 87

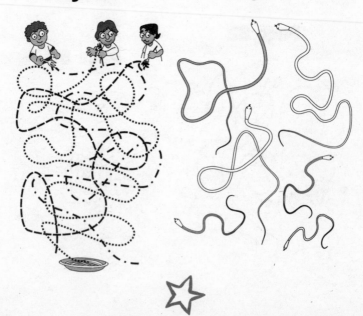

☆

Page 88

Page 89

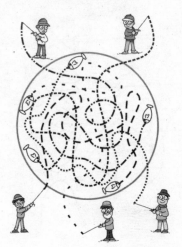

Page 90

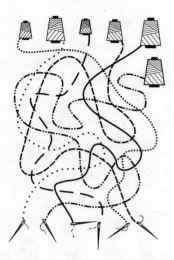

Page 91

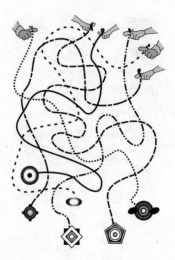

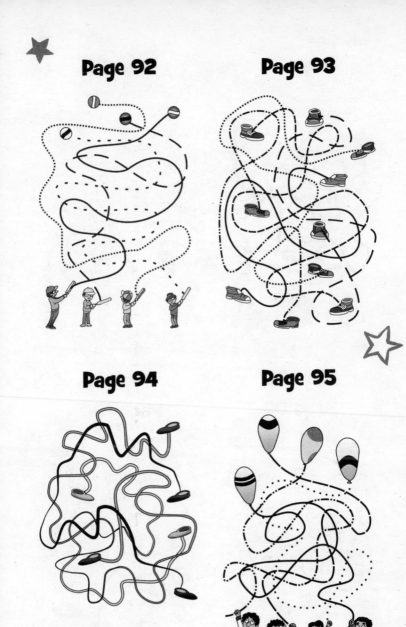

Page 92

Page 93

Page 94

Page 95

Page 96 **Page 97** **Page 98**

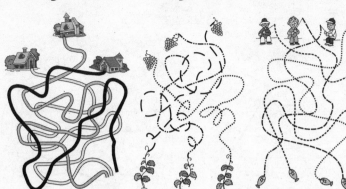

★ FRACTAL MAZES

Page 99 **Page 100**

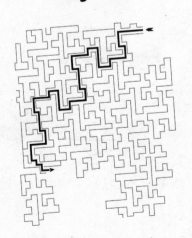

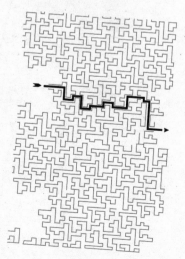

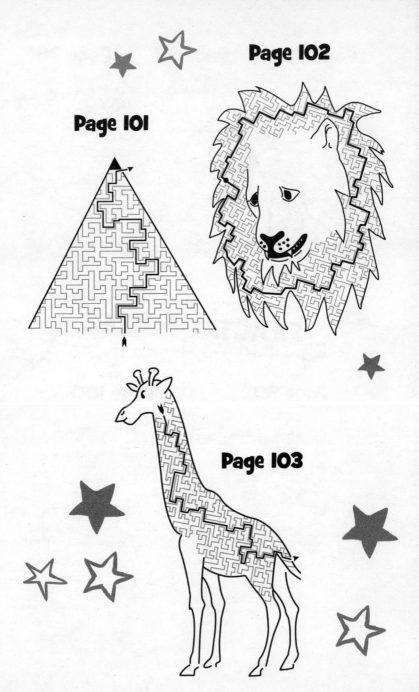

Page 101

Page 102

Page 103